The Declaration of Independence

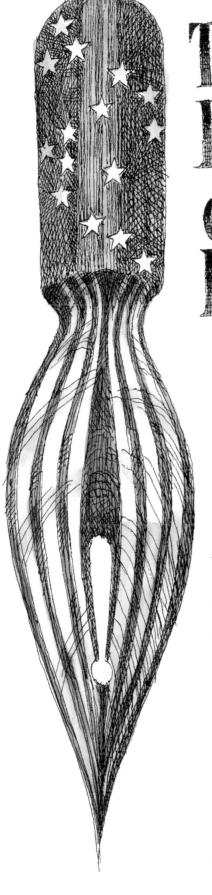

The Declaration of Independence

Illustrated and Inscribed by Sam Fink

SCHOLASTIC NONFICTION

Library of Congress Cataloging-in-Publication Data

United States. ★ The Declaration of Independence / inscribed and illustrated by
Sam Fink; text by Thomas Jefferson ★   p. cm. ★ Includes bibliographical
references (p.). ★ Summary: The text of the Declaration of Independence
is accompanied by illustrations meant to help explain its meaning. ★ 1. United
States. Declaration of Independence—Juvenile literature. 2. United States—
Politics and government—1775-1783—Juvenile literature. [1. United States.
Declaration of Independence.] I. Jefferson, Thomas, 1743-1826. II. Fink,
Sam, ill. III. Title. ★ E221 .U57 2002 ★ 2001058194 ★ 0-439-40700-1

10 9 8 7 6 5 4 3   02 03 04 05 06

★ PRINTED IN THE U.S.A. ★
First printing, July 2002

Additional text by Elysa L. Jacobs
Curriculum consultation by Bob Stremme
Lexicographical review by John K. Bollard
Art direction by Nancy Sabato
Colorization by Greg Paprocki

★   ★   ★

To Mirjam and David and Gertrude.

Contents

JOSIAH BARTLETT · WILLIAM WHIPPLE
MATTHEW THORNTON · SAMUEL HUNTINGTON
ROGER SHERMAN · WILLIAM WILLIAMS

OLIVER WOLCOTT · SAMUEL ADAMS · JOHN ADAMS
ROBERT TREAT PAINE · ELBRIDGE GERRY
STEPHEN HOPKINS · WILLIAM ELLERY

JOHN HANCOCK · GEORGE TAYLOR · WILLIAM FLOYD
PHILIP LIVINGSTON · FRANCIS LEWIS · LEWIS MORRIS
ROBERT MORRIS · BENJAMIN RUSH

BENJAMIN FRANKLIN · JOHN MORTON · GEORGE CLYMER
JAMES SMITH · JAMES WILSON · GEORGE ROSS
RICHARD STOCKTON · JOHN HART

FRANCIS HOPKINSON · ABRAHAM CLARK
WILLIAM PACA · CHARLES CARROLL OF CARROLLTON
JOHN WITHERSPOON · GEORGE READ
SAMUEL CHASE · CAESAR RODNEY
THOMAS STONE ·

GEORGE WYTHE · RICHARD HENRY LEE · THOMAS JEFFERSON
THOMAS McKEAN · FRANCIS LIGHTFOOT LEE
BENJAMIN HARRISON · THOMAS NELSON, Jr.
· CARTER BRAXTON ·

JOHN PENN · BUTTON GWINNETT
WILLIAM HOOPER · JOSEPH HEWES · THOMAS LYNCH, Jr.
LYMAN HALL · GEORGE WALTON · EDWARD RUTLEDGE · ARTHUR MIDDLETON
THOMAS HEYWARD, Jr. ·

The names of the 56 men who pledged
to each other their Lives, their Fortunes,
their sacred Honor for an Independent America.

For as long as I can remember,

every Fourth of July *The New York Times* reproduced a copy of the original Declaration of Independence on the back page. Each time it appeared, I would look it over with admiration and go out to celebrate like multitudes of Americans. Parades to enjoy, barbecues to feast on, fireworks to watch.

A couple of years ago, I thought I would actually try to read it. Old eyes and illegible script made it very difficult. A borrowed book from the local library, containing all the words neatly printed, came to the rescue. Reading it over several times, enjoying it more and more, I became very impressed with Thomas Jefferson's logic. I liked his argument of how unfairly the colonies were being treated, how they couldn't stand it anymore, and how they needed to break away from Great Britain. So, I planned a project...

I would divide the text of the Declaration into short phrases or sentences, hand lettering the words on one page and illustrating the ideas expressed by those words on the facing page. Once I started working, the project sort of took off on its own.

The work filled my days with energy and great pleasure. Then came the big surprise when I submitted it to Scholastic——they decided to publish it. What excitement! With the guidance of editors and an art director, the book has come to life.

The words that made America can now be shared with people of all ages; and they can help us understand what the Founding Fathers created for all of us who have followed. Freedom . . . oh, sweet freedom.

Sam Fink
GREAT NECK, NY

On the 7th of June 1776, the Second Continental Congress met in Philadelphia. Richard Henry Lee of Virginia proposed a resolution to declare the thirteen Colonies free and independent of Britain. On the 11th of June, a committee of five was appointed to write a Declaration.

Tho' **Jefferson**

John Adams

Benj' **Franklin**

Roger Sherman

RR **Livingston**

This was the committee. What follows is what they wrote: The glorious Declaration of Independence, unanimously proclaimed on the 4th of July 1776.

hen
in the Course
of human events,

it becomes necessary for one people to dissolve the political bands which have connected them with another,

and to assume among the powers of the earth, the separate and equal station to which the Laws of Nature and of Nature's God entitle them,

a decent respect
to the opinions of mankind
requires that they should
declare the causes
which impel them
to the separation.

We sing of Liberty, Freedom and Independence

e hold these truths
to be self-evident, that
all men are created equal,
that they are endowed
by their Creator
with certain
unalienable Rights,

that among these
are Life, Liberty
and the pursuit
of Happiness.

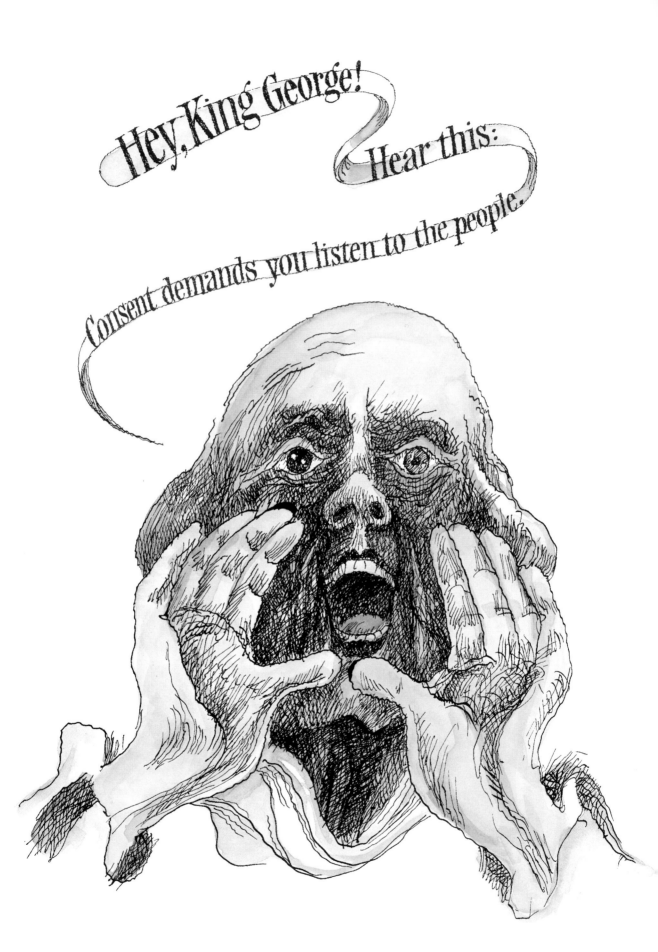

That to secure these rights, Governments are instituted among Men, deriving their just powers from the consent of the governed,

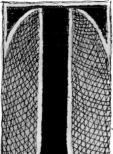

That whenever any
Form of Government
becomes destructive
of these ends,
it is the Right
of the People
to alter
or to abolish it,

nd
to institute
new Government,

laying
its foundation
on such principles
and organizing its powers
in such form, as to them
shall seem most likely
to effect their Safety
and Happiness.

Peace
Safety
Security
Reliability
Solid
Foundation
Home as a
Private Castle
Out of Harm's Way
Security
Representation
in Government

Prudence, indeed,
will dictate
that Governments
long established
should not be changed
for light and
transient causes;

And accordingly
all experience hath shewn,
that mankind
are more disposed
to suffer, while evils
are sufferable,

than

to right themselves
by abolishing
the forms to which
they are accustomed.

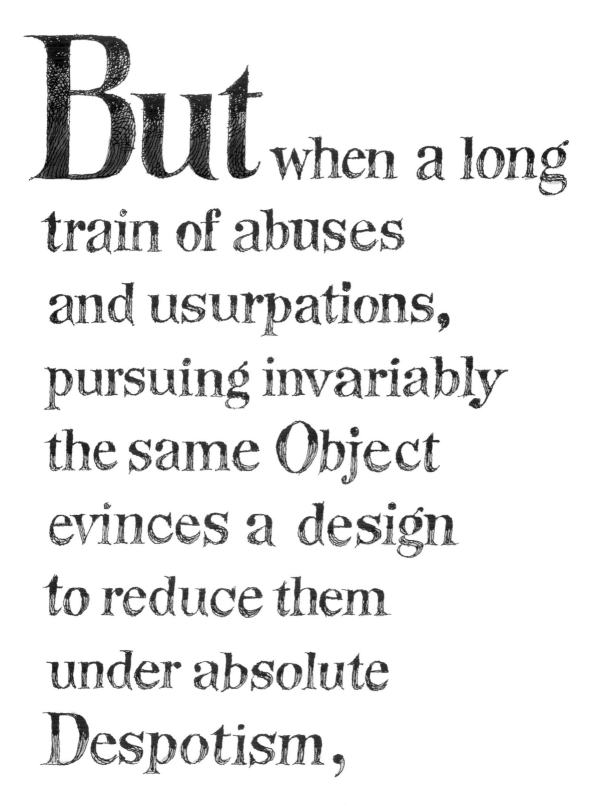

But when a long train of abuses and usurpations, pursuing invariably the same Object evinces a design to reduce them under absolute Despotism,

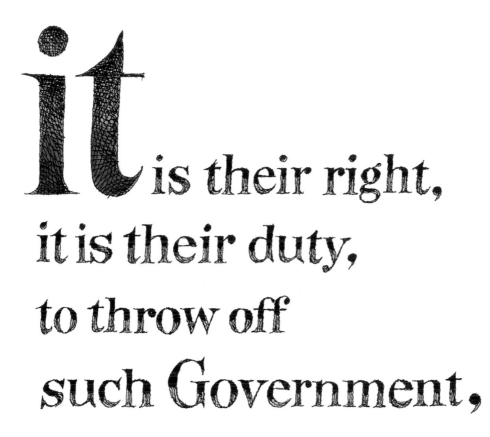

it is their right,
it is their duty,
to throw off
such Government,

and

to provide
new Guards
for their
future security.

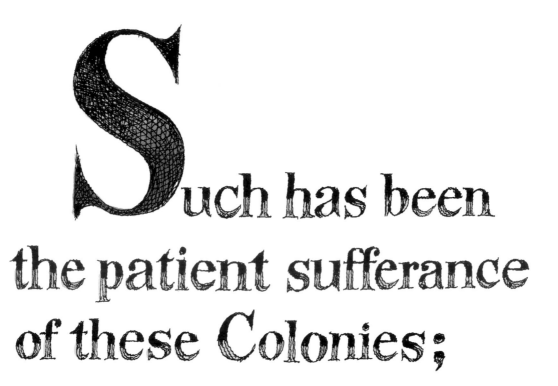

Such has been
the patient sufferance
of these Colonies;

and
such is now the necessity which constrains them to alter their former Systems of Government.

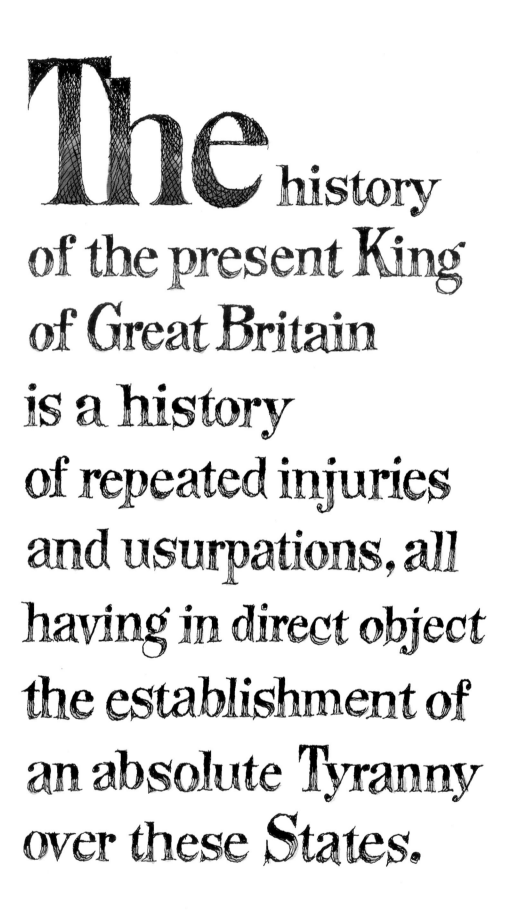

The history of the present King of Great Britain is a history of repeated injuries and usurpations, all having in direct object the establishment of an absolute Tyranny over these States.

tyrant (tī′rənt) n. An absolute ruler who governs arbitrarily without constitutional or other restrictions. A ruler who exercises power in a harsh, cruel manner.

49

To prove this, let Facts be submitted to a candid world.

He has refused his Assent to Laws, the most wholesome and necessary for the public good.

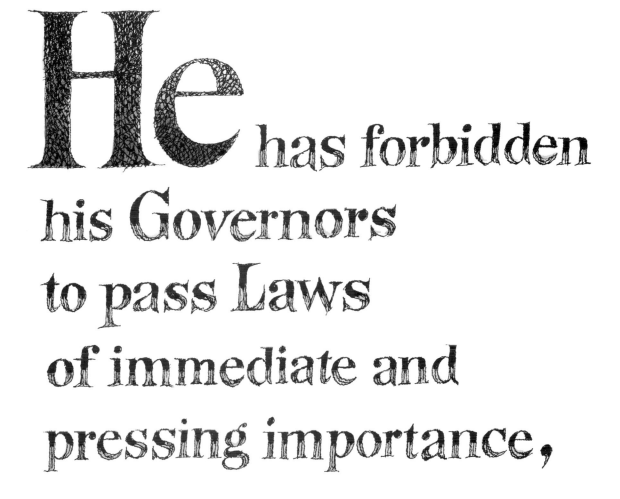

He has forbidden his Governors to pass Laws of immediate and pressing importance,

unless

suspended
in their operation
till his Assent
should be
obtained;

**when so suspended,
he has utterly neglected
to attend to them.**

1. New Hampshire
2. Massachusetts
5. New York
3. Rhode Island
4. Connecticut
7. Pennsylvania
6. New Jersey
8. Delaware
9. Maryland
10. Virginia
11. North Carolina
12. South Carolina
13. Georgia

N
W   E
S

He has refused to pass other Laws for the accommodation of large districts of people,

unless

those people would
relinquish the right
of Representation
in the Legislature,
a right inestimable
to them
and formidable
to tyrants
only.

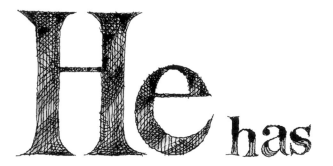

He has
called together
legislative bodies
at places unusual,
uncomfortable,
and distant
from the depository
of their
public Records,

Enter here to get to the King's meeting place.

the sole purpose
of fatiguing them
into compliance
with his measures.

He has dissolved
Representative
Houses repeatedly,
for opposing
with manly firmness
his invasions
on the rights
of the people.

He has refused
for a long time,
after such dissolutions,
to cause others
to be elected;

71

whereby

the Legislative powers,
incapable of
Annihilation, have
returned to the
People at large for
their exercise;

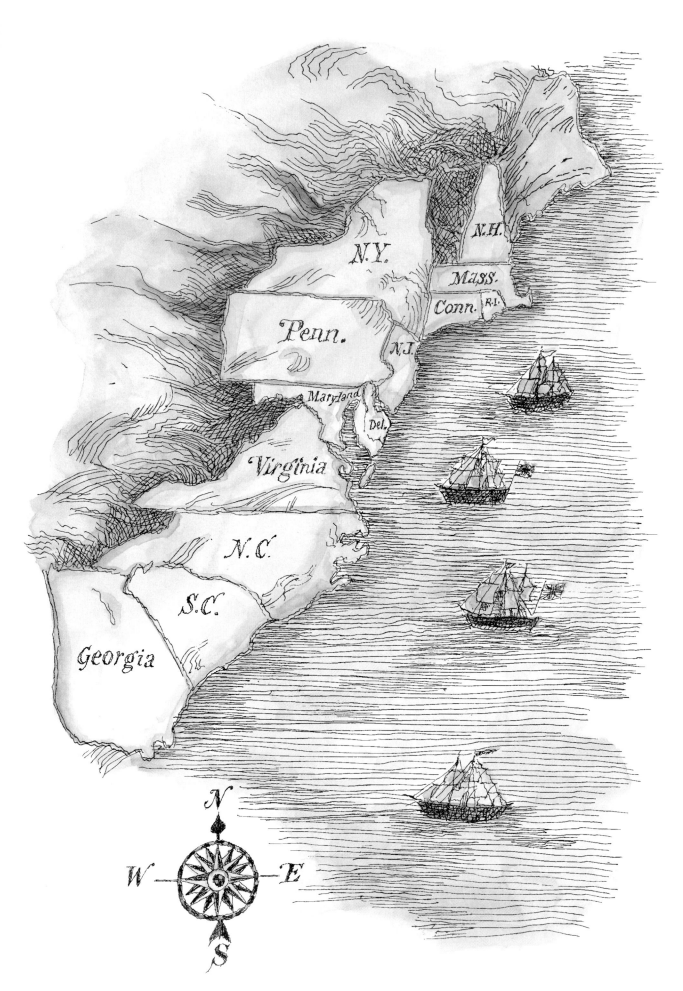

N.Y.

N.H.

Mass.

Conn. R.I.

Penn.

N.J.

Maryland

Del.

Virginia

N.C.

S.C.

Georgia

N

W E

S

the State

remaining in the mean time exposed to all the dangers of invasion from without, and convulsions within.

The King's rope of frustration

He has
endeavoured
to prevent
the population
of these States;
for that purpose
obstructing the
Laws for Naturalization
of Foreigners;

refusing

to pass others
to encourage
their migrations hither,
and raising
the conditions of
new Appropriations
of Lands.

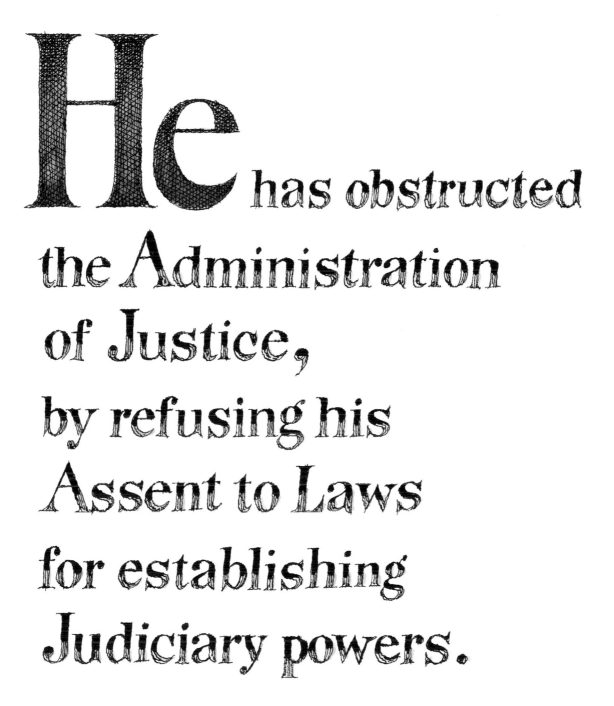

He has obstructed the Administration of Justice, by refusing his Assent to Laws for establishing Judiciary powers.

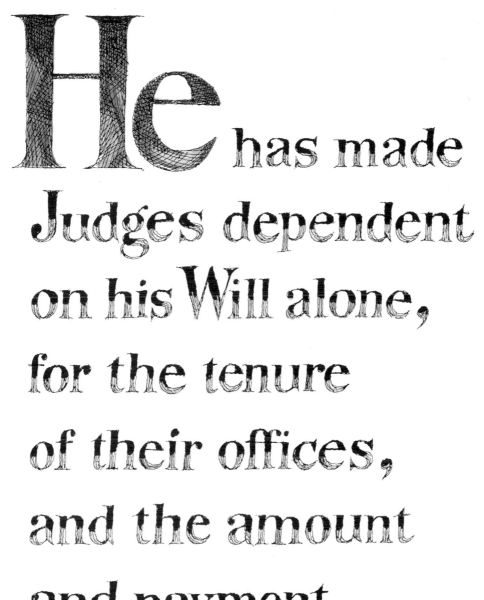

He has made Judges dependent on his Will alone, for the tenure of their offices, and the amount and payment of their salaries.

The King's Multitude of New Offices:

The Office for This

The Office for That

The Office of NOW

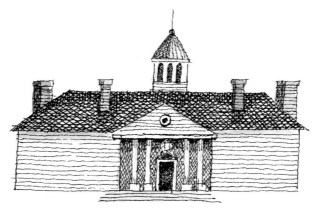

The Office of THEN

The Office of What?

The Office of When?

The Office of Where?

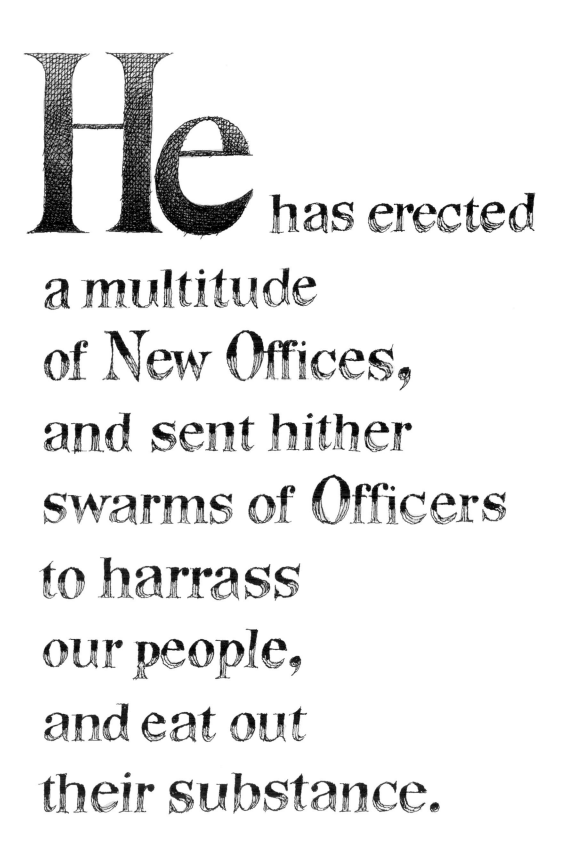

He has erected
a multitude
of New Offices,
and sent hither
swarms of Officers
to harrass
our people,
and eat out
their substance.

He has kept among us, in times of peace, Standing Armies without the Consent of our legislatures.

He has affected
to render the Military
independent of
and superior
to the Civil power.

He has combined
with others to subject
us to a jurisdiction
foreign to
our constitution,
and unacknowledged
by our laws;
giving his Assent
to their Acts
of pretended
Legislation:

Easy living!

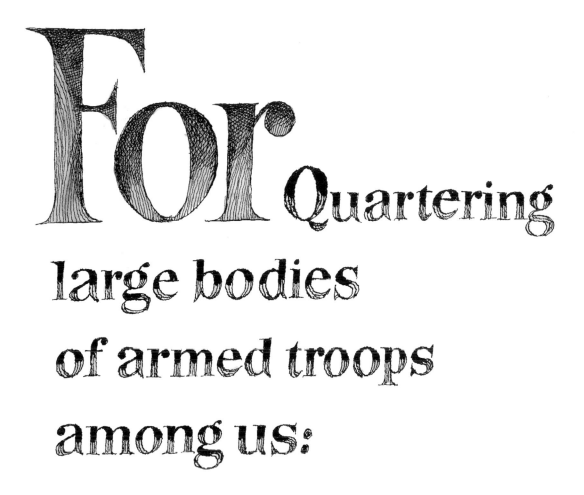

For Quartering large bodies of armed troops among us:

For protecting them, by a mock Trial, from punishment for any Murders which they should commit on the Inhabitants of these States:

The King is outrageous!

For cutting off our Trade with all parts of the world:

For imposing Taxes on us without our Consent:

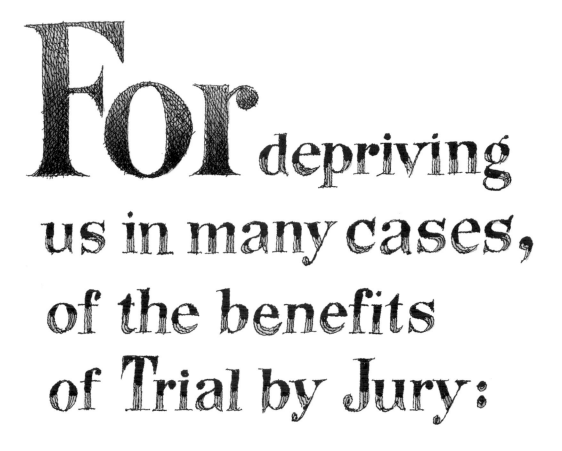

For depriving us in many cases, of the benefits of Trial by Jury:

For transporting us beyond Seas to be tried for pretended offences

a neighbouring Province,
establishing therein an
Arbitrary government,
and enlarging
its Boundaries so as
to render it at
once an example
and fit instrument
for introducing
the same
absolute rule
into these Colonies:

For taking away our Charters, abolishing our most valuable Laws,

and altering
fundamentally
the Forms of
our Governments:

For suspending our own Legislatures, and declaring themselves invested with power to legislate for us in all cases whatsoever.

He has abdicated Government here, by declaring us out of his Protection and waging War against us.

He has
plundered our seas,
ravaged our Coasts,
burnt our towns,
and
destroyed the lives
of our people.

Unworthy?

I'll show them unworthy!

He is

at this time transporting
large Armies of
foreign Mercenaries
to compleat
the works of death,
desolation and tyranny,

already begun
with circumstances
of Cruelty & perfidy
scarcely paralleled in
the most barbarous ages,
and totally
unworthy the Head
of a civilized nation.

He has constrained our fellow Citizens taken Captive on the high Seas to bear Arms against their Country,

I am the enemy!

No, I am the enemy!

to become the executioners of their friends and Brethren, or to fall themselves by their Hands.

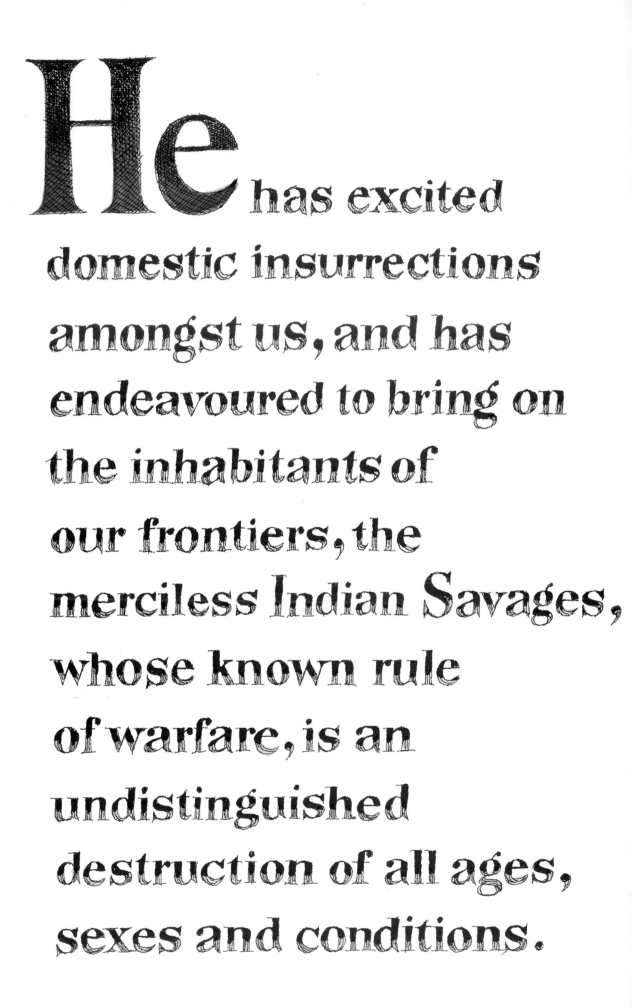

He has excited domestic insurrections amongst us, and has endeavoured to bring on the inhabitants of our frontiers, the merciless Indian Savages, whose known rule of warfare, is an undistinguished destruction of all ages, sexes and conditions.

In every stage of these Oppressions We have Petitioned for Redress in the most humble terms: Our repeated Petitions have been answered only by repeated injury.

A Prince
whose character
is thus marked
by every act
which may define
a Tyrant, is unfit
to be the ruler
of a free people.

Nor have
We been wanting
in attentions to
our British brethren.
We have warned them
from time to time
of attempts
by their legislature
to extend
an unwarrantable
jurisdiction over us.

We have
reminded them
of the circumstances
of our emigration
and settlement here.

We have appealed
to their native justice
and magnanimity, and
we have conjured them
by the ties of
our common kindred
to disavow
these usurpations,
which, would inevitably
interrupt our connections
and correspondence.

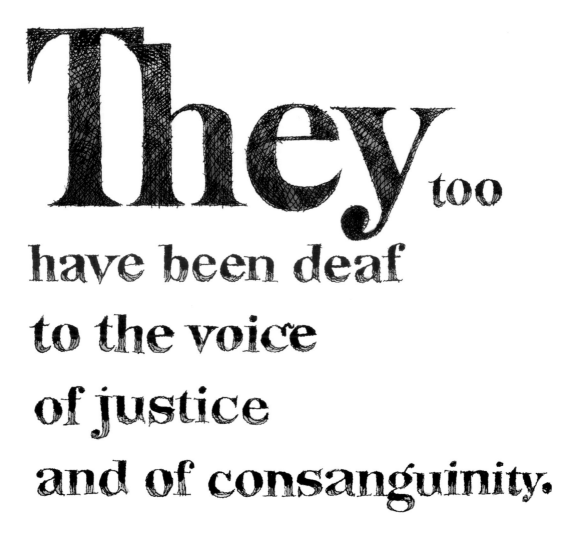

They too
have been deaf
to the voice
of justice
and of consanguinity.

131

We must, therefore, acquiesce in the necessity, which denounces our Separation, and hold them, as we hold the rest of mankind, Enemies in War, in Peace Friends.

We,

therefore,
the Representatives of the
united States of America,
in General Congress,
Assembled, appealing
to the Supreme Judge
of the world
for the rectitude
of our intentions,

do, in the Name, and by Authority of the good People of these Colonies, solemnly publish and declare, That these United Colonies are, and of Right ought to be Free and Independent States;

are Absolved
from all Allegiance
to the
British Crown,

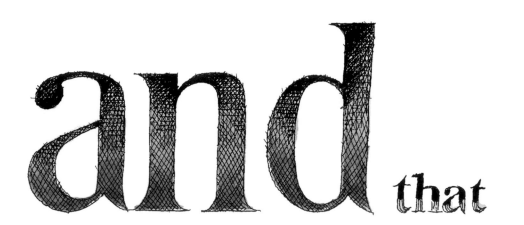

and that
all political connection
between them and
the State of Great Britain,
is and ought to be
totally dissolved;

that as
Free and Independent States,
they have full Power
to levy War,
conclude Peace,
contract Alliances,
establish Commerce,
and to do all other Acts
and Things which
Independent States
may of right do.

And
for the support
of this Declaration,
with a firm reliance
on the protection
of divine Providence,
we mutually pledge
to each other
our Lives, our Fortunes
and our sacred Honor.

The Declaration of Independence

IN CONGRESS, July 4, 1776.

The unanimous Declaration of the thirteen united States of America,

WHEN IN THE COURSE OF HUMAN EVENTS, it becomes necessary for one people to dissolve the political bands which have connected them with another, and to assume among the powers of the earth, the separate and equal station to which the Laws of Nature and of Nature's God entitle them, a decent respect to the opinions of mankind requires that they should declare the causes which impel them to the separation.

We hold these truths to be self-evident, that all men are created equal, that they are endowed by their Creator with certain unalienable Rights, that among these are Life, Liberty and the pursuit of Happiness. That to secure these rights, Governments are instituted among Men, deriving their just powers from the consent of the governed, That whenever any Form of Government becomes destructive of these ends, it is the Right of the People to alter or to abolish it, and to institute new Government, laying its foundation on such principles and organizing its powers in such form, as to them shall seem most likely to effect their Safety and Happiness. Prudence, indeed, will dictate that Governments long established should not be changed for light and transient causes; and accordingly all experience hath shewn, that mankind are more disposed to suffer, while evils are sufferable, than to right themselves by abolishing the forms to which they are accustomed. But when a long train of abuses and usurpations, pursuing invariably the same Object evinces a design to reduce them under absolute Despotism, it is their right, it is their duty, to throw off such Government, and to provide new Guards for their future security.

Such has been the patient sufferance of these Colonies; and such is now the necessity which constrains them to alter their former Systems of Government. The history of the present King of Great Britain is a history of repeated injuries and usurpations, all having in direct object the establishment of an absolute Tyranny over these States. To prove this, let Facts be submitted to a candid world.

He has refused his Assent to Laws, the most wholesome and necessary for the public good.

He has forbidden his Governors to pass Laws of immediate and pressing importance, unless suspended in their operation till his Assent should be obtained; and when so suspended, he has utterly neglected to attend to them.

He has refused to pass other Laws for the accommodation of large districts of people, unless those people would relinquish the right of Representation in the Legislature, a right inestimable to them and formidable to tyrants only.

He has called together legislative bodies at places unusual, uncomfortable, and distant from the depository of their public Records, for the sole purpose of fatiguing them into compliance with his measures.

He has dissolved Representative Houses repeatedly, for opposing with manly firmness his invasions on the rights of the people.

He has refused for a long time, after such dissolutions, to cause others to be elected; whereby the Legislative powers, incapable of Annihilation, have returned to the People at large for their exercise; the State remaining in the mean time exposed to all the dangers of invasion from without, and convulsions within.

He has endeavoured to prevent the population of these States; for that purpose obstructing the Laws for Naturalization of Foreigners; refusing to pass others to encourage their migrations hither, and raising the conditions of new Appropriations of Lands.

He has obstructed the Administration of Justice, by refusing his Assent to Laws for establishing Judiciary powers.

He has made Judges dependent on his Will alone, for the tenure of their offices, and the amount and payment of their salaries.

He has erected a multitude of New Offices, and sent hither swarms of Officers to harrass our people, and eat out their substance.

He has kept among us, in times of peace, Standing Armies without the Consent of our legislatures.

He has affected to render the Military independent of and superior to the Civil power.

He has combined with others to subject us to a jurisdiction foreign to our constitution, and unacknowledged by our laws; giving his Assent to their Acts of pretended Legislation:

For Quartering large bodies of armed troops among us:

For protecting them, by a mock Trial, from punishment for any Murders which they should commit on the Inhabitants of these States:

For cutting off our Trade with all parts of the world:

For imposing Taxes on us without our Consent:

For depriving us in many cases, of the benefits of Trial by Jury:

For transporting us beyond Seas to be tried for pretended offences

For abolishing the free System of English Laws in a neighbouring Province, establishing therein an Arbitrary government, and enlarging its Boundaries so as to render it at once an example and fit instrument for introducing the same absolute rule into these Colonies:

For taking away our Charters, abolishing our most valuable Laws, and altering fundamentally the Forms of our Governments:

For suspending our own Legislatures, and declaring themselves invested with power to legislate for us in all cases whatsoever.

He has abdicated Government here, by declaring us out of his Protection and waging War against us.

He has plundered our seas, ravaged our Coasts, burnt our towns, and destroyed the lives of our people.

He is at this time transporting large Armies of foreign Mercenaries to compleat the works of death, desolation and tyranny, already begun with circumstances of Cruelty & perfidy scarcely paralleled in the most barbarous ages, and totally unworthy the Head of a civilized nation.

He has constrained our fellow Citizens taken Captive on the high Seas to bear Arms against their Country, to become the executioners of their friends and Brethren, or to fall themselves by their Hands.

He has excited domestic insurrections amongst us, and has endeavoured to bring on the inhabitants of our frontiers, the merciless Indian Savages, whose known rule of warfare, is an undistinguished destruction of all ages, sexes and conditions.

In every stage of these Oppressions We have Petitioned for Redress in the most humble terms: Our repeated Petitions have been answered only by repeated injury. A Prince whose character is thus marked by every act which may define a Tyrant, is unfit to be the ruler of a free people.

Nor have We been wanting in attentions to our British brethren. We have warned them from time to time of attempts by their legislature to extend an unwarrantable jurisdiction over us. We have reminded them of the circumstances of our emigration and settlement here. We have appealed to their native justice and magnanimity, and we have conjured them by the ties of our common kindred to disavow these usurpations, which, would inevitably interrupt our connections and correspondence. They too have been deaf to the voice of justice and of consanguinity. We must, therefore, acquiesce in the necessity, which denounces our Separation, and hold them, as we hold the rest of mankind, Enemies in War, in Peace Friends.

We, therefore, the Representatives of the united States of America, in General Congress, Assembled, appealing to the Supreme Judge of the world for the rectitude of our intentions, do, in the Name, and by Authority of the good People of these Colonies, solemnly publish and declare, That these United Colonies are, and of Right ought to be Free and Independent States; that they are Absolved from all Allegiance to the British Crown, and that all political connection between them and the State of Great Britain, is and ought to be totally dissolved; and that as Free and Independent States, they have full Power to levy War, conclude Peace, contract Alliances, establish Commerce, and to do all other Acts and Things which Independent States may of right do. And for the support of this Declaration, with a firm reliance on the protection of divine Providence, we mutually pledge to each other our Lives, our Fortunes and our sacred Honor.

MASSACHUSETTS:
John Hancock
Samuel Adams
John Adams
Robert Treat Paine
Elbridge Gerry

GEORGIA:
Button Gwinnett
Lyman Hall
George Walton

NORTH CAROLINA:
William Hooper
Joseph Hewes
John Penn

SOUTH CAROLINA:
Edward Rutledge
Thomas Heyward, Jr.

Thomas Lynch, Jr.
Arthur Middleton

MARYLAND:
Samuel Chase
William Paca
Thomas Stone
Charles Carroll of Carrollton

VIRGINIA:
George Wythe
Richard Henry Lee
Thomas Jefferson
Benjamin Harrison
Thomas Nelson, Jr.
Francis Lightfoot Lee
Carter Braxton

PENNSYLVANIA:
Robert Morris
Benjamin Rush

Benjamin Franklin
John Morton
George Clymer
James Smith
George Taylor
James Wilson
George Ross

DELAWARE:
Caesar Rodney
George Read
Thomas McKean

NEW YORK:
William Floyd
Philip Livingston
Francis Lewis
Lewis Morris

NEW JERSEY:
Richard Stockton

John Witherspoon
Francis Hopkinson
John Hart
Abraham Clark

NEW HAMPSHIRE:
Josiah Bartlett
William Whipple
Matthew Thornton

RHODE ISLAND:
Stephen Hopkins
William Ellery

CONNECTICUT:
Roger Sherman
Samuel Huntington
William Williams
Oliver Wolcott

Chronology

Below you will find a list of the events that transformed loyal subjects of Great Britain into rebellious, patriotic Americans.

★ 1748 ★ The Spirit of Laws

Charles de Montesquieu publishes a book called *The Spirit of Laws*, in which he writes about different types of government. He describes the importance of keeping the three branches of government—executive, judicial, and legislative—separate. (Some of de Montesquieu's ideas are expressed in the Declaration of Independence.)

★ 1762 ★ The Social Contract

Jean Jacques Rousseau publishes an essay called *The Social Contract*. The essay describes Rousseau's theory that a country's government will only remain powerful as long as the people who are governed support it. If a government turns into a tyranny, the citizens may unite and withdraw their support of the government. Without the support of the people, a government is powerless. (The Founding Fathers of the United States were impressed by Rousseau's writing, which is evident in the Declaration of Independence and United States' Constitution.)

★ 1763 ★ *Proclamation of 1763*

King George III issues the Proclamation of 1763. The proclamation states that colonists should not settle on land that lies west of the Appalachian Mountains. King George wants the western land to continue to belong to the Native Americans. He does not want colonists to fight with the Native Americans about the land, possibly starting a long expensive war. Many colonists are angered by the proclamation because they do not want limits placed on where they may travel and settle.

★ 1764 ★ *The Sugar Act*

Parliament (the lawmaking body of England) passes the Sugar Act (also called the American Revenue Act). The act places a tax on sugar, coffee, and other imported goods. This is the first time Parliament tries to tax the colonists. The money raised from the tax will be used to pay for the British soldiers stationed throughout the colonies. The soldiers are there to protect the colonists from foreign invasions. There is a great deal of protest against the Sugar Act. Colonists claim it is unlawful for Parliament to tax them when they have no representation in Parliament. (This is where the phrase "taxation without representation" comes from.)

★ 1765 ★ The Stamp Act

Parliament passes the Stamp Act on March 22. This law requires people to pay a tax to Great Britain each time certain printed materials, such as wills, marriage licenses, playing cards, newspapers, and magazines, are issued. Colonists are angered by this most recent example of taxation without representation.

★ 1766 ★ Repeal of the Stamp Act

On March 18, Parliament makes two important decisions. First, the Stamp Act is repealed due to a great deal of protest from the colonists. Second, the Declaratory Act is passed. In this act, Parliament gives itself total authority to govern the colonies in any manner. When the colonists learn of Parliament's actions, they celebrate the repeal of the hated Stamp Act but pay little attention to the Declaratory Act.

★ 1767 ★ The Townshend Acts

Parliament passes the Townshend Acts on June 29. The acts place duties (taxes) on such goods as tea, paper, lead, paint, and glass imported from Great Britain. Again, the colonists protest this attempt to tax them unfairly. They go to great lengths to avoid paying the duties; men and women make tea from homegrown plants and smuggle in goods from other countries.

★ 1768 ★ British Soldiers Arrive in Boston

On October 1, thousands of British soldiers arrive in Boston, Massachusetts. Their assignment is to prevent any further rebellion from colonists. Citizens resent the presence of a permanent army during a time of peace. They are also angry that they must help feed and house the British soldiers.

★ 1770 ★

MARCH ~ The Boston Massacre On March 5, an angry group of colonists threatens the British soldiers. As a result, the soldiers fire their guns into the crowd and five colonists die. This event quickly becomes known as the "Boston Massacre."

APRIL ~ The Townshend Acts Repealed Parliament repeals all Townshend duties except those on tea. The tea tax is left in place to show the colonists that Parliament and King George III have the right to rule the colonies however they wish.

★ 1773 ★ The Tea Act and the Boston Tea Party

On April 27, Parliament passes the Tea Act of 1773. This act forces the colonists to buy tea from England and pay the tea tax. Colonists actively protest the Tea Act by throwing hundreds of chests of British tea into Boston Harbor on December 16. This event is known as the Boston Tea Party.

★ 1774 ★

MAY – The Intolerable Acts In response to the Boston Tea Party, Parliament passes new laws to prevent further revolt in Boston. Known in the colonies as the Intolerable Acts, these laws include closing the port of Boston to all trade and allowing British officials accused of committing a crime in the colonies to be taken back to Great Britain for a trial.

SEPTEMBER TO OCTOBER – First Continental Congress As a result of the Intolerable Acts, each colony appoints delegates to attend a congress (meeting) to discuss the colonies' situation with Great Britain. The First Continental Congress meets from September 5 to October 26 in Philadelphia, Pennsylvania. Representatives from all the colonies (except Georgia, which is very far away) attend to make a list of the colonies' grievances against King George III and Parliament. The colonists formally state their unhappiness with the Intolerable Acts and the presence of a standing army. The delegates want the acts and the soldiers to be removed.

★ 1775 ★

APRIL – The Ride of Paul Revere On April 18, Paul Revere makes his famous midnight ride from Boston to Lexington, warning of the approach of British soldiers. Revere alerts Samuel Adams and John Hancock, two important patriots, that the British are planning to march to Concord to seize control of a militia store of weapons.

APRIL – "The Shot Heard 'Round the World" On April 19, the first battle of the American Revolution occurs in Lexington, Massachusetts. British soldiers were passing through Lexington in order to reach Concord. A single gunshot (it is unknown to this day who fired first) is heard, triggering a short exchange of gunfire. As a result, eight patriots die, and ten more are wounded. Only one British soldier is injured.

MAY – Second Continental Congress On May 10, the Second Continental Congress begins to meet in Philadelphia. Many colonial representatives are still reluctant to completely dissolve the ties between the colonies and Great Britain.

JUNE – George Washington Appointed Commander-in-Chief On June 15, the Second Continental Congress appoints George Washington commander-in-chief of the newly formed Continental Army.

JULY TO AUGUST ~ Official Rebellion In July, the colonists send the Olive Branch Petition to King George. They hope he will finally pay attention and help resolve their complaints. Without reading the petition, the king declares that the colonies are officially in rebellion.

★ 1776 ★

JANUARY ~ **Common Sense** Thomas Paine writes *Common Sense*. The pamphlet is read by tens of thousands of colonists. In it, Paine outlines the reasons why the colonies should declare independence from Great Britain. Throughout 1776, the colonies notify the Continental Congress that they would support a declaration of independence.

JUNE ~ Richard Henry Lee's Resolution On June 7, Richard Henry Lee of Virginia brings a resolution to the Second Continental Congress that states that the thirteen colonies should be "free and independent States. . . ."

JUNE ~ Jefferson Begins Drafting the Declaration of Independence While the members of the Second Continental Congress debate the pros and cons of independence, a committee is created on June 11. This group will draft a document that, if used, would declare the colonies' independence from Great Britain. The committee in charge of drafting a declaration was Benjamin Franklin of Pennsylvania, Robert Livingston of New York, John Adams of Massachusetts, Roger Sherman of Connecticut, and Thomas Jefferson of Virginia.

Thomas Jefferson spends about two weeks writing the first draft of the Declaration of Independence.

JULY ~ The Continental Congress Adopts the Declaration of Independence

★ On July 2, the Second Continental Congress approves Richard Henry Lee's resolution.
★ On July 3, Congress debates the text of the Declaration of Independence.
★ On July 4, the Second Continental Congress adopts the Declaration of Independence. It is signed by John Hancock, president of Congress, and Charles Thomson, the Congress secretary. (July 4 is celebrated every year as the United States' birthday.)
★ On July 8, the Liberty Bell is rung in Philadelphia to bring people to the State House. The Declaration of Independence is read to the public for the first time. Colonists celebrate everywhere the Declaration is proclaimed.
★ On July 19, the Continental Congress orders the Declaration to be engrossed (written in fancy handwriting) on parchment. All fifty-six members sign this document, making it official.

Glossary

The words listed below can be found in the text of the Declaration of Independence or in the illustrations in this book. Some of the words in the Declaration had different meanings in 1776 than they do now. Others words may be new to you or may be spelled or used in a way you are not familiar with. When you come across a word you don't know, look below and replace it with the meaning given on the right. The meanings will help you understand what the Founding Fathers meant.

abdicated done away with; rejected

abolish do away with; put an end to

absolute complete

absolved set free

accommodation convenience; benefit

acquiesce in accept

administration performance

affected tried

allegiance loyalty

alter change

annihilation complete destruction

appealed asked for understanding and sympathy

appropriations purchases

arbitrary not controlled by laws or authority

assent official acceptance

assume take as a right

attend to consider; give attention to

bands connections

barbarous uncivilized; savage

brethren brothers

bring on cause to fight against

candid open-minded; fair; impartial

circumstances (1) events; incidents (2) facts and details relating to an event

civil power the power of the people and their government, not military power

commerce business; trade

compleat complete

compliance agreement

conclude settle; decide on

conditions requirements

conjured requested in a serious manner

consanguinity relationship by descent from the same ancestors consent agreement or permission

constitution customs and laws

constrains forces; compels

convulsions violent conflicts

correspondence communication

course the path of something through time

decent proper and polite

declaration a serious statement or announcement

denounces formally announces in public

depository a place where important items are kept

depriving taking away from

deriving obtaining; receiving

design plan

desolation destruction

despotism a government with a leader who rules with unlimited power

disavow state one's disapproval of

disposed inclined; likely

dissolutions the dismissal or breaking up of groups

dissolve end; destroy

dissolved dismissed; put an end to

divine Providence God

domestic relating to the country or area in which a person lives

effect bring about

emigration leaving one's country of origin to move to a new country

endeavoured tried

endowed...with given

entitle give someone a legal right to something

evinces reveals; shows

excited stirred up; brought about

executioners those who put others to death

exercise use

fatiguing exhausting; tiring

fit suitable

foreign to completely inappropriate for

formidable causing fear or alarm

fundamentally in basic and important ways

harass cause trouble for

hath shewn has shown

hither to this place

impel push; force

imposing forcing us to accept

incapable of not able to do or achieve

inestimable extremely valuable; priceless

inevitably in a way that cannot be avoided; unavoidably

inhabitants people who live in a given area

instituted organized; established; created

insurrections revolts

intentions plans; goals

invariably constantly

invested with possessing; holding

judiciary relating to judges and courts of law

jurisdiction a system of justice

kindred family relationship; kinship

Laws of Naturalization of Foreigners laws that describe how people from other countries can move to and become official residents of a new country or place

legislate make laws

legislation the making of laws

legislative lawmaking

legislature a group of people with the power to make laws

levy make

light unimportant

magnanimity generosity

manly courageous

measures proposed laws

mercenaries soldiers for hire

migrations acts of moving from one place to settle in another

mock fake; false

object goal; purpose
  in direct object as a specific goal

obstructing blocking; opposing

obtained gotten; acquired

oppressions acts of cruelty

perfidy disloyalty and betrayal

petitioned formally asked

petitions formal requests

plundered used force to steal from

population the increase of the number of people

powers (1) states; nations
  (2) authority

pressing calling for immediate attention; urgent

prince ruler

proclaimed announced publicly

prudence good judgment

public good the benefit of the entire population of a given area

publish announce officially

pursuing trying to get or achieve something

pursuit the action of trying to get or achieve something

quartering housing

raising increasing

ravaged caused great damage to

rectitude correctness

redress correction of or repayment for something wrong

reduce bring under control; conquer

reliance the state of depending or relying on someone

relinquish give up

render declare; make

resolution an official statement by a group of an opinion or idea

right make things right for

scepter a staff, carried by a king or queen, that represents the power he or she has

secure make safe; protect

self-evident understood without explanation or evidence

sole single, only

solemnly seriously

standing permanent

station position

substance belongings; property

sufferable bearable; endurable

sufferance putting up with a difficult situation with patience

suspended stopped for a period of time

tenure the right or authority to hold a particular job

therein in that place

trade exchange of goods; business

transient existing only for a short period of time

transporting carrying; shipping

tyranny oppressive and unjustly harsh government

tyrant a powerful ruler, especially one who is unjust and cruel

unacknowledged not recognized

unalienable that cannot be taken away or removed

unanimously without anyone disagreeing

undistinguished without exception

unwarrantable unjustified

unworthy not worthy of

usurpations acts of wrongfully taking away someone's rights or property

waging making

wanting lacking

whatsoever no matter what

whereby as a result; therefore

wholesome helpful; healthful

Selected Bibliography

The following sources were used to create the chronology:

Corn, Ira G. *The Story of the Declaration of Independence: Illustrated and Documented*. New York: Pinnacle Books, 1977.

Hammerman, Gay M. and Trevor N. Dupuy, eds. *People & Events of the American Revolution*. Dunn Lorring, Virginia: T. N. Dupuy Associates, 1974.

Hoehling, Mary, and Betty Randall. *For Life and Liberty: The Story of the Declaration of Independence*. New York: Julian Messner, 1969.

Ross, George E. *Know Your Declaration of Independence and the 56 Signers*. Chicago: Rand McNally, 1963.

Selected Resources

SUGGESTIONS FOR FURTHER READING

Bober, Natalie S. *Countdown to Independence: Revolution of Ideas in England and Her American Colonies, 1760–1776*. New York: Simon & Schuster, Atheneum, 2001.

Freedman, Russell. *Give Me Liberty!: The Story of the Declaration of Independence*. New York: Holiday House, 2000.

Marrin, Albert. *George Washington and the Founding of a Nation*. New York: Penguin Putnam, Dutton Children's Books, 2001.

Masoff, Joy. *American Revolution, 1700–1800*. New York: Scholastic, 2000.

Moore, Kay. *If You Lived at the Time of the American Revolution*. New York: Scholastic, 1998.

Roop, Connie, and Peter Roop. *Betsy Ross*. New York: Scholastic, 2002.

Roop, Connie, and Peter Roop. *Benjamin Franklin*. New York: Scholastic, 2001.

Sullivan, George. *Paul Revere*. New York: Scholastic, 2000.

WEB SITES

National Archives and Records Administration
To find out where the Declaration of Independence is housed today, go to the Web site below. Once there, you'll not only see pictures of the original Declaration and a stone engraving of the document, but you'll also find out about the steps being taken to preserve this important piece of American history.
http://www.nara.gov/exhall/charters/charters.html

Library of Congress
Looking through the Library of Congress Web site will reveal some additional information about the Declaration of Independence. Included there is another transcription of the Declaration as well as links to other documents that played important roles in the founding of our nation.
http://memory.loc.gov/const/mdbquery.html

Independence Hall Association
This Web site contains a great deal of information about the men who wrote and signed the Declaration. You can find everything from biographical information about all 56 signers to sections of Thomas Jefferson's autobiography that describe the time leading up to the signing of the Declaration.
http://www.ushistory.org/declaration/

Index

Page numbers in italics indicate illustrations.

Illustrator's Note

I have long been an admirer of the *Declaration of Independence* and I wanted to make it as beautiful as I could in this book. To do so, I used a simple Roman typeface to hand letter the text of the Declaration. The shape and size of the letters reminds me of the primers I used to learn to read when I was in grade school. I felt that the simplicity of the typeface would allow the text to speak for itself. Thomas Jefferson's words are powerful and need no further embellishment from me.

For a previous book I wrote and illustrated, I did a great deal of research on the 56 men who signed the Declaration. In the process, I learned a lot about the way people in the late 1700s dressed. Although the style of the clothing on the people in this book is accurate, the clothes' colors are lighter and more playful than those the men would have actually worn. Most of the men who signed the Declaration wore clothes that were often darker, and more somber looking, than they appear in my illustrations.

As I began to hand letter the text of the Declaration, I noticed that depending on which source I looked at, the punctuation and capitalization were different. In one version a word would start with a capital letter, in another it would start with a lowercase letter.

To be consistent, I chose to follow the style in the Declaration transcription from the National Archives and Records Administration.

Working on this project has been a wonderful experience and I hope that you enjoy exploring the Declaration of Independence as much as I have.